# Walking in Love:
## My Journey along the Camino de Santiago

Roy W. Howard

Parson's Porch Books

*Walking in Love: My Journey along the Camino de Santiago*
ISBN: Softcover 978-1-951472-17-7
Copyright © 2016 by Roy W. Howard

All rights reserved. No part of this book may be reproduced or transmitted in any form or by any means, electronic or mechanical, including photocopying, recording, or by any information storage and retrieval system, without permission in writing from the publisher.

To order additional copies of this book, contact:

Parson's Porch Books
1-423-475-7308
www.parsonsporch.com

Parson's Porch Books is an imprint of Parson's Porch & Company (PP&C) in Cleveland, Tennessee. PP&C is an innovative company which raises money by publishing books of noted authors, representing all genres. All donations from contributors and profits from publishing are shared with the poor.

*Walking in Love*

# Acknowledgements

I am grateful for the congregation and the leaders of Saint Mark Presbyterian Church in North Bethesda Maryland who provided the sabbatical that made possible my pilgrimage. They remain unfailing in their support and prayer for their pastor. I'm also grateful for my staff colleagues Shelby Etheridge Harasty, Jeff Doenges, Ron Wolfe and Christina Steffanelli who carried on beautifully in my absence.

My Camino pilgrims from around the world: thank you for such rich conversations that revealed the wide bounds of God's love beyond all narrow confines.

Laura Todd provided much needed editorial assistance and encouragement for this project. I may not have persevered without her gentle nudging me forward. Lynn McClintock gave us helpful suggestions on the photo selection.

At sunrise my fellow pilgrim Meg Holmes took a photograph of me walking up to the Cruz de Ferro. She and I had a wonderful Camino moment as dawn broke over the mountain. Her photograph is on the cover.

My wife Claudia and our daughters, Rachel and Rebecca, know me better than anyone on the planet. Yet, grace upon grace, they continue to love me, laugh with me, pray for me, encourage me and support me in the adventures of the Spirit. I can't imagine life without them.

*Bless the Lord, O my soul, and forget not all God's benefits. Psalm 103:2*

# The Gift of Love
## 1 Corinthians 13

If I speak in the tongues of mortals and of angels,
but have not love, I am a noisy gong or a clanging cymbal.
And if I have prophetic powers,
and understand all mysteries and all knowledge,
and if I have all faith, so as to remove mountains,
but do not have love,
I am nothing.
If I give away all my possessions,
and if I hand over my body so that I may boast,
but have not love, I gain nothing.

Love is patient, love is kind.
It does not envy, it does not boast, it is not proud.
It does not dishonor others, it is not self-seeking, it is not easily angered,
it keeps no record of wrongs.
Love takes no delight in evil, but rejoices in the truth.
Love bears all things,
believes all things,
hopes all things,
endures all things.
Love never ends.

But as for prophecies, they will come to an end;
as for tongues, they will cease;
as for knowledge, it will come to an end.
For we know only in part, and we prophesy only in part;
but when the complete comes, the partial will come to an end.
When I was a child, I spoke like a child, I thought like a child,
I reasoned like a child;
when I became an adult, I put an end to childish ways.
For now we see in a mirror, dimly,
but then we will see face to face.
Now I know only in part; then I will know fully, even as I have been fully known. And now faith, hope, and love abide, these three;
and the greatest of these is love.

# Prologue

**The journey** begins in a French village at the base of the Pyrenees Mountains and ends in a Spanish village overlooking the Atlantic Ocean. In between is a path that millions of pilgrims have walked since the 12th century. In the spring of 2015, I was one of them, on sabbatical from my pastorate. The way is known as the Camino de Santiago de Compostela, a 500-mile path over the mountains and across northern Spain. Modern pilgrims are a mixed company of many languages, some traditionally religious and others non-religious, though walking with an explicit and often spiritual intent. I didn't walk as a religious penitent seeking absolution from my sins. I did walk with a purpose. I wanted to listen closely for God's direction, particularly for the next chapter of my life. I also wanted to be radically free from my normal patterns to see my life from a fresh angle.

This is the story of what occurred as I walked this path with a remarkable company of pilgrims from all over the world. My daily observations are recorded here, along with a few chants and scriptures that guided my way and deepened my intentions.

The poet Wendell Berry said, "Always in the big woods when you leave familiar ground and step into a new place there will be … a little nagging of dread. It is the ancient fear of the Unknown, and it is your first bond with the wilderness you are going into. What you are doing is exploring. You are undertaking the first experience, not of the place, but of yourself in that place." From the first day I crossed the mountains, walking through snow and rain in the bitter cold, the Camino became an exploration of self-understanding in an utterly new place. *The freedom was exhilarating.* The sense of the Unknown and the nagging dread remained with me, along with the company of pilgrims who became my Camino family. Several remain so.

Daily at dawn, I would arise from my bunk bed, place my belongings in a small backpack, and walk out the door. The Camino winds through wide valleys and small villages, among vineyards and the vast grasslands of the high plains. It crosses the rugged mountains of Galicia before descending to Santiago. The spring flowers are breathtaking, especially the acres of brilliant red tulips on the hills. Bird songs are abundant, including the ubiquitous call of the cuckoo. Most days, I didn't know what I would eat, where I would sleep, or whom I would meet. I had a wondrous sense of being on the edge of fear and faith.

Daily I prayed, "I will receive this day with gratitude and an open heart." Sharing simple meals with bread and wine, engaging in slow, honest conversations that frequently reached rare spiritual depth, tending the pains of one another — the Camino is a profound communal experience of conviviality. In nearly every village, there is a daily mass for the pilgrims who greet each other with "*Buen Camino,*" roughly translated "Enjoy your walk." The response is "*Ultreïa et Suseia,*" a Latin/French/Spanish word of encouragement that means something like "Keep going forward [into God.]"

I reached Santiago de Compostela in 31 days, celebrating joyously with my Camino family. Two days later, I walked on to Finisterre, the village on the coast of Spain known as the end of the world. Here the original pilgrims faced the ocean, literally the end of the road, where the world ends and the unknown begins. When I began my pilgrimage, I did not know fully what to expect or what would happen. How it continues to unfold in my life remains an occasion for wonder and gratitude.

# The Beginning
May 20, 2016

**Day 1**

The journey begins in St. Jean Piet de Port on the border of France and Spain in the Basque country. My intention is to walk *(live!)* in a mind-ful manner. **Lord, you know my heart; teach me your way (Psalm 86).**

I began walking with Jeff Krehbiel, his sister Janet, and their friend Jean Stewart. Jeff is my friend and clergy colleague who initially encouraged me to walk. He is also on sabbatical. We left at 6 a.m., and after a very steep climb, I arrived at 10 a.m. at the Refugio Orisson where we had reservations for the night. It was cold and rainy, but my energy level was very high. At this moment, I decided to walk on and cross the Pyrenees into Roncesvalles, Spain. I walked with Simon Strauss, a young German graduate student, 15.3 miles with a 4,300-foot elevation gain, through rain, hail, and wind in the low 40s. Griffon Eagles, common in the Pyrenees, were soaring, and I also saw Laxta bighorn sheep. Took a pretty hard trek and am now at the hostel at the Monastery in Roncesvalles. Grateful. I guess I'm really walking solo now, and that is an exhilarating feeling! Hope to see Jeff, Janet, and Jean along the way.

**Day 2**
Roncesvalles to Larrasoana. 27.5K (17 mi.).

Today, the Camino went through beautiful forests and valleys. We were serenaded the whole day with bird songs. The early spring flowers lined the path most of the way. It was quite cool in the morning, perfect for walking through the forest. It seems as though I am journeying with the whole world through these relationships and conversations with my fellow pilgrims from Australia, Denmark, South Africa, Germany, Canada, France, South Korea, Holland, Switzerland, Ireland, the United States, and Colombia. Today, my prayer focus/chant is hope, the virtue and practice of it, especially that hope will fill the hopeless. I met a Colombian woman, Aleida, who gladly translated my chant into Spanish so that I could sing it in English and Spanish. Perhaps, before it's over, I'll have many languages singing in my heart. We will all share dinner tonight at the simple albergue (hostel). It feels like the whole world coming together over a meal and I'm filled with gratitude.

**Day 3**
Larrasoana to Pamplona. 16K, *only* 9 miles today.

The Camino went along the Arga River much of the morning and through more urban areas before arriving in Pamplona, the largest city along the Camino. This is the city made famous by the running of the bulls and Ernest Hemingway. Staying at Casa Paderborn, run by an older German couple, Herman and Gertrude. My suite mates are all Koreans! It cost only 8.5 euros including breakfast. I had long stretches of solitude while walking, except for the extraordinary singing birds. It's a good thing I didn't bring my binoculars, I would never arrive at the destination! The Griffon Eagles continue to soar all along the way. My prayer focus/chant today is love: for God, neighbor, self, and enemy. All day long, this mantra: God is love, and those who live in love live in God. As I was walking and chanting my mantra, an old man across the field with his dogs waved exuberantly to me, saying "Buen Camino, peregrino!" At this moment, my heart spontaneously cracked open. I was reduced to weeping, not from sorrow or sadness, but something else, maybe love, maybe gratitude. I'm still weeping in wonder of it all.

**Day 4 - (Faith)**
Pamplona to Puente la Reina. 24K (15 miles.)

Only at an albergue managed by a German couple in Pamplona will I rise at 6 a.m. to six Korean and Australian roommates in a house filled with opera music! The Camino passed through Pamplona on a steady incline across a ridge at the highest point, Alto del Perdón, where the wind is fierce. No surprise the ridge is lined with modern windmills. Cool in the morning (60 degrees Fahrenheit) and warm with sun in the afternoon (70 degrees). Today had an Irish theme. I walked much of the way with a recent college graduate, Ciara, from Dublin. She studied art history and English literature/poetry. I mentioned W.B. Yeats, and she quoted a lovely poem, "He Wishes for the Cloths of Heaven," which she interprets as being about treading kindly on the earth. When I asked if she was doing this walk for religious or spiritual reasons, she said "I can't really say I'm religious, though I was raised Catholic, and I don't know if I'm spiritual." "And what will you do at home?" I asked. "I'm lost," she replied. "There is no job for an art history/English major. So I'm walking until my money runs out." We walked along quietly for a while and will continue to cross paths as we make our way to Santiago. When I arrived at Puente de la Reina, I searched with a pilgrim from Holland for a place to stay. Finally, after three closures, we found a place. There, I had a conversation with my roommate from Malaysia. She is on leave from work.

My prayer focus/chant today is Faith. "Faith is the assurance of things hoped for; the conviction of things not yet seen" (Hebrews 11:1). ***We are taught to seize the day (Carpe diem!) but I am learning to receive the day, without control or management, being present to what comes as gift into this one beautiful day. This is a singular moment for me; one with has deep and lasting importance.***

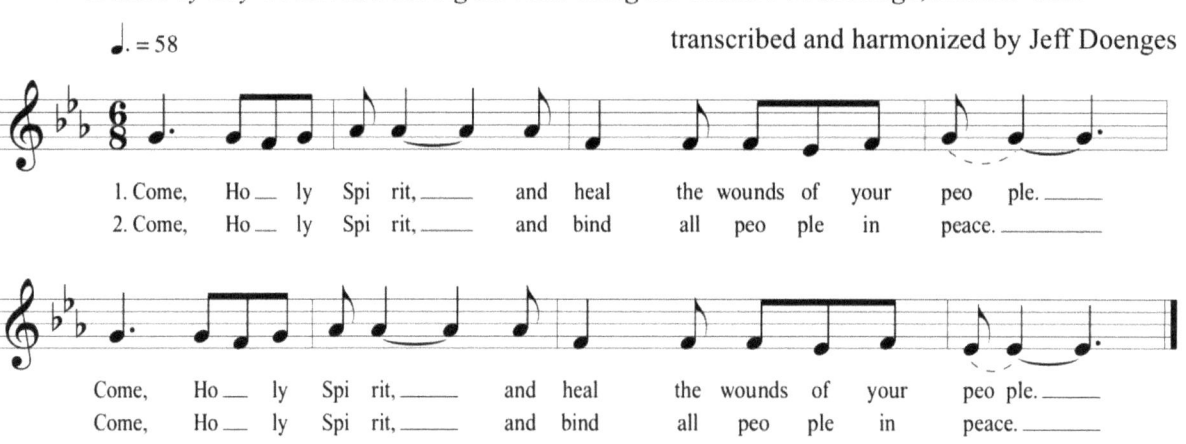

**Day 5 (Spirit)**
Puente de la Reina to Estella. 24.8 K (15 miles).

It's a sunny day, and by the end of the walk quite hot. I put on a long-sleeved wick dry shirt for skin protection--very important! The Camino rolls along up and down through fields of wheat, lined with spring flowers. Stunning beauty. I finally saw the bird that has been serenading the peregrinos all along the way. A warbler with an orange chest and black cap perched on a branch long enough for me to see. I also heard a cuckoo! Started the day walking with a man from Hong Kong and a woman from Holland. Ended the day with a man from South Africa whom I met on the first day. There are more people limping along the Camino, some in great pain. Today being Pentecost, the prayer focus/chant is Spirit. *Veni Sancte Spiritus* (Come Holy Spirit). As I passed over the Puente la Reina, I saw a sign inviting people to Pentecost mass: "Hay diversidad de dones, pero un mismo Espiritu" (There are varieties of gifts, but the same Spirit).

As I walked along, surrounded by beauty and the languages of people from all over the world, my chant/song was "*Come Holy Spirit. Fill the hearts of all people with peace. Come Holy Spirit. Heal the wounds of your world. Come Holy Spirit. Bind us together in peace.*" My feet and legs are holding up fine, a bit sore at the end of the daily walk but okay after a rest. (see song here)

**Day 6 (Spirit 2)**
Estella to Los Arcos. 22K (14 miles).

What a beautiful day of walking across wheat fields and wineries. The temperature was perfect, in the 70s with sun and cloud cover. I started the day early, walking with a peregrino from Belgium; we enjoyed a drink at Irache wine fountain a few kilometers before Estelle (the earliest I've had wine!). Then, I walked much of the day in solitude, with occasional conversations as people pass along the Camino. I'm finding myself spontaneously weeping as I walk and chant/sing/pray because the beauty is so astonishing every step along the way. I don't know exactly what the weeping is about, but I'm just receiving what is coming my way with joy without trying to contain or explain it. At about 12 miles, my feet began slow lamentation. The mental training of several marathons is becoming quite a gift. I arrived in the little village of Los Arcos with a man from Ireland walking with his daughter. After finding an albergue, I went to the plaza and shared conversation with peregrinos from Holland, Belgium, South Africa, and California. One of my roommates had torn the skin from his foot and can barely walk. He asked if I trained and I said yes, of course. He replied that he did no training, his pack was too heavy, and he was out of shape. I doubt he will continue. What puzzles me is why so many pilgrims have not trained for this pilgrimage and neglect such basic care of their feet. Today's prayer chant focused on the Fruit of the Spirit as described in Galatians: "'Love, joy, peace, patience, kindness, goodness, faithfulness, humility, and self-control.' Let the fruit of your Spirit grow in me."

**Day 7 (Patience-Long suffering)**
Los Arcos to Logroño. 28 K (17.5 mi.)

The Camino moved along through wheat fields and wine country with strikingly beautiful vistas. About one-fourth of the way was on asphalt and near a roadway as we moved toward Logroño, the capital of the winemaking region of La Rioja. The temperature in the early hours was 12°C (53°F) with sun and clouds, perfect for walking. I'm learning as I go to receive the day as it comes to me rather than predict it. A young peregrino from Hong Kong, Nick, walked alongside me. He quit his job two years ago and has been hiking much of that time. He said he wanted to discover something more than money. He asked me why I was walking, and I told him: adventure, challenge, discernment, conversation, and prayer. That was a puzzle to him. "So you just pray to something you like?" I said, "I'm a pastor. A Christian." He asked, "What is a pastor?" So I explained pastor. He then said "I don't like Christians judging others as bad; I'm Buddhist; but I like the idea of forgiveness and new birth." I said, *"I'm not judging you, but if you like the idea of forgiveness and new birth, you might like Jesus too. I'm trying to walk in Jesus' way, and I think the Buddha would like that."* He smiled a big smile. "I like talking with you," he said. Then, he walked on at a 27-year-old pace.

I smiled too. At the approach to Logroño, I saw a stork soaring over a field. Wonderful sight. Then, I saw the mother stork in her nest feeding three baby storks. Wow. What a great way to end a 17-mile walk! My prayer focus/chant for the next several days is on the Fruits of the Spirit. "May the fruit of your Spirit grow in me: patience, long-suffering." And "Come Holy Spirit. Heal the wounds of your people. Bind all peoples in peace." It has been a good day. Now having a glass of wine from this famous region. I have walked 200 kilometers (124 miles) this week. There are 600 kilometers to Santiago!

**Day 8 (Humility)**
Logroño to Nájera. 29 K (18.5 mi.)

So today's walk was long and in perfect weather. I had the happy occasion of walking the entire stage with Clara from Barcelona, who gave me a full history of Catalonia and its relationship to Spain (she's a freelance journalist who also works as a tour guide in Barcelona). Most Americans don't know the distinctions between Castilian Spain, Basque, and Catalonia. Now I know this distinction very well. Clara has walked the Camino four times. She describes herself as no longer a practicing Catholic yet having a sense of something transcendent, larger than mere materialism. This is a common theme of those walking the Camino. We shared quite personal stories of what this "sense of the transcendent" might mean theologically and practically as we walked 18 miles through the vineyards of La Rioja. I'm enjoying this simple sharing of stories. It's expanding my mind and heart. The conversation with Clara, a non-practicing Christian, was remarkably theological. I wonder if this is the only way in which "God talk" can occur across differences. We concluded the day with a dinner and conversation with pilgrims from four different continents. My prayer focus/chant was on the gift of humility. "Let the fruit of your Spirit grow in me."

**Day 9 (Kindness)**
Nájera to Grañón. 27K 16 miles.

This was quite an amazing day in addition to the beauty surrounding us as we walked through vineyards and wheat fields, serenaded by various sparrows and wrens. After arriving in the village of St. Domingo, Clara insisted we visit the local Cathedral where live chickens are kept commemorating a miracle. (The Roman Catholic culture of Spain is filled with these fantastical miracle stories. Truth and fiction are bound closely together. It reminds me of Gabriel García Márquez' fictional universe.) After we entered the village and had settled in our simple albergue, Clara heard of this wonderful church in the next village, Grañón, where a true community occurs among the pilgrims. So we gathered up our packs and walked 7K (4.5 miles) down the way under very intense sun. I'm so glad we did! Wow. It's a simple place -- we sleep on the floor with mats -- but the Camino volunteers do everything to make this a communal experience even though there are many people from various traditions.

We all shared in the preparation of the meal, from setting up the tables to chopping the potatoes, onions, and carrots. It all happened in a spontaneous choreography with a wondrous cacophony of languages. Those who wanted to went to a mass/Eucharist with a prayer/benediction for peregrinos from the parish priest. Leaving the sanctuary, we gathered outside for singing and conviviality with wine, bread, and chorizo (pork sausage). Some had their feet tended to by a pilgrim skilled in the treatment of blisters. In the rustic dining room, we sat together for a meal of bread, salad, and stew that we had prepared and our hosts had finished. Again, there was such rich conversation in variety of languages.

**For me, it was the Church embodied.**

While this is not the church in any technical sense, the hospitality, warmth, and kindness enacted here is the Church embodied in such a universal way that even those who are not Christians experience the actual community that God intends for all people. Among those gathered around the table were people from Hungary, New Zealand, Canada, Uruguay, Catalonia, Italy, France, Germany, Spain, Korea, Colombia, England, and the U.S. My heart filled up with a profound sense of *hilaritas* and gratitude. Some of us concluded the evening with a prayer service and reflection in the choir loft of the cathedral, with silence and praying in various languages. We then retired to our mats on the floor, as lights were out at 10:30 p.m., to awake at 6:30 a.m. for breakfast. The prayer/chant/song today focused of the Fruit of the Spirit, kindness. "Let the fruit of your Spirit grow in me: kindness."

**Day 10 (Goodness)**
Grañon to Villambistia. 31K (19 miles)

A gentle journey up and down through wheat fields and mostly alongside the road. Still occasionally stricken by bursts of tears of gratitude and joy, today while singing a little chant that I created from a fragment of verse by Antonio Machado, a Barcelona poet: "There is no Way/We make the way by walking. / There is a Way/We make the way by walking/ Con tus amigos, con tus amigas y con Dios" (repeat). Perhaps I'll have a musician make it melodious enough for community singing. In any event, these moments of tears are pure gift. I walked a long way today with a French peregrino, Jean Christophe, the father of two adolescent children. I asked my common question, "Why are you walking?" He said, "*I have many reasons, but maybe I don't exactly know. I am doing this to discover more of who I am, and I think my children understand only this reason. It's for my health because I am a sick man.*" I thought this last reason was a joke, but no; he has diabetes. He began to describe his fortieth birthday party a few days before he started walking, in which he asked his friends to choose the music for his funeral. We had a rich conversation about his experience of the death of religion in his life as a habitual Roman Catholic who finally realized that it had no meaning for him. It is not the loss of God, he said, but the loss of any connection to his life and that of his family. He played organ for a small parish church that he described as "only for old women who listen to old priests say old things, while young people find more life in a bar." "So why are you walking?" I asked. "I don't know for sure; it's the right time. For a sense of inner accomplishment and maybe to find meaning, adventure, and even God too." He moved on as my German friend and I stopped at an albergue in a town with a population of 47. I had conversation with a young man from Hungary there. The prayer chant today focused on goodness. "Let the fruit of your Spirit grow in me: goodness."

**Day 11 (Peace)**
Villambistia to Cardeñuela Riopico 31K (19 miles)

The Camino went up and up gently until around 4,000 feet and then along a ridge most of the way. I passed through forests with pine trees mostly but even through a couple of Aspen glades. Again, the weather was strikingly beautiful, cool in the morning and sunny as the day went on. I walked much of the day alone. That is a particular learning for me. It's wondrous, (and slightly fearful) to put my belongings on my back at sunrise, not knowing what (or where) I will eat, whom I will meet, or where I will stay, with faith that I will indeed have something to eat, a place to stay, and people to meet along the way. I walk out with my morning chant: "I will receive this day with gratitude and an open heart." As this day unfolds, I am ready to receive what comes as gift.

Today, I realize that I *enjoy* walking alone when I'm in the company of others, knowing we will "hang together" at the end of the day. **But I find it unsettling to be walking alone without anyone and with no knowledge of where I will stay. This is a sweet spot of insight. Today, it occurs to me that this is where faith meets fear.** I walk on alone in the trust that I will have a place to stay, food to eat, and perhaps people to meet. I went one town further than I anticipated and indeed found a place to stay in a nice albergue. Surprise! There, I met a peregrino that I last saw five days ago. She was having a crisis of confidence at that very moment, considering abandoning the journey. Our conversation occurred precisely at that moment. It was rich and helpful. Now, we shall walk together tomorrow with my South African friend Oscar and Holgar, a friend from Germany, both of whom have been companions from the first day. I find this an amazing gift that I did not anticipate in any way. Is this what it means to *receive* the day? There is a steady flow of pilgrims into my life for a few hours or even days, then a shift occurs, a pace or a plan changes, and they are gone. *I want to live into this pattern of receiving and letting go without trying to force or manipulate it.*

So what else? I heard many birds, and they even showed themselves to me: a small warbler with an orange throat, a vireo with eye ring, (similar to a White-Eyed Vireo), a wren with a black and white eye mask, a stork, and a cuckoo; all in all, a remarkable day. I wish I had my bird book and binoculars. But, again, if I did I might never reach the destination! My prayer focus/chant is peace. I'm learning to live precisely in the moment as it comes and, when it comes, give thanks.

**Day 12 (Trinity Sunday)**
Cardeñuela Riopico to Burgos. 13.2K (8 miles)

This was a short walk to the city of Burgos by the alternative route by the river and through a lovely city park that is the largest park I've ever walked; probably 2.5 miles long. Burgos is a beautiful city with a great tree-lined avenue. Lots of people out and about for Sunday holiday when all the stores are closed and people gather in the plazas for tapas and conviviality. In Spain, tapas can be practically anything-- from a chunk of tuna, a cocktail onion and an olive skewered on a long toothpick, to piping hot chorizo sausage served in a small clay dish, to a gourmet slow-cooked beef cheek served over a sweet potato puree - or anything in between. You may have noticed that my favorite word is *conviviality*: the quality of friendliness and good-hearted joy. It is here in abundance.

My continuing sense is that the European cities are more conducive to community by their design of plazas, squares, and open spaces for people to gather. My traveling companions are from Germany and Arizona. We will meet others from Ireland, Hong Kong, Colombia, South Africa, Oklahoma, and Texas for dinner in the main plaza near the Cathedral de Burgos, which, by the way, is an astonishing architectural feat. I'm not real keen on gold-laden churches, but this place, built in the 12th and 13th centuries, is truly amazing. It is a UNESCO World Heritage site. We took the tour of the massive place. Then, we went to the cultural museum for a special exhibit covering 100 years of Spanish artists, a really fine museum. All in all, it has been a good way to spend Trinity Sunday.

Remember the person having a crisis of confidence yesterday? She is walking with us, doing much better, and lo and behold, another peregrina friend experiencing a similar crisis read my Facebook post, contacted me, and is now going to join up with us for some companionship*. I believe that is the way the Spirit creates community in real life.*

**Day 13 (Joy)**
Burgos to Hontanas 31K (19 mi.)

This was a long stretch over the Meseta (high plains) under cloudless sky. The temperature reached 31°C (87°F). A kind older man escorted us out of Borges at 6:45 a.m. across the city, pointing out highlights as we eventually reached the Camino. At first, I thought him annoying, but then I came to my senses! In his exuberance, he was offering a gesture of kind hospitality to a couple of strangers. And he was certainly helping me with my Spanish! Out of the city, we walked across the high plains at an elevation of 2,000 feet, wheat field after wheat field as far as the eye can see. I walked the day with a peregrino from Arizona, a nurse practitioner. Leisurely, we talked of all manner of things, sharing our stories. This is another gift of the Camino. After walking 19 miles in blazing heat, it was great to find an albergue as we entered the village. We are sharing a room with a mother and daughter from North Carolina, a mother and daughter from Austria, one man from Germany, and another from Ireland. We'll share dinner with all of them and a couple of guys from Canada tonight. Such an ordinary day of blessing! As of today, I have walked 322K (200 miles). For the sake of honesty and your curiosity, my feet are sore at the end of this day, and my left little toe is in some slight pain. All shall be well. The prayer focus is joy. "Let the Fruit of the Spirit grow in me: joy." (A fellow peregrino wore a bright orange shirt emblazoned with "Today I choose joy!")

**Day 14 (Faithfulness)**
Hontanas to Boadilla del Camino 28.5K (17.7 mi.)

The day began at 6:45, as we began to leave the albergue when our new NC friends discovered that someone had left with the mother's walking boots! Holy Toledo! I would be nuts. She was calm and accepted her reality with remarkable peace. The rest of us were amazed. She must now go back to Burgos to purchase new boots and begin again. "It's only a little blip along the way," she says. Her college-aged daughter will go on and meet her at an arranged destination. For a day devoted to "faithfulness," this was a great lesson. My current traveling companion, the nurse practitioner from Arizona, had rich conversation about just what faithfulness means in practice. She is not a church person and commented at length on why that is so, including the superficiality she has encountered again and again in Christian worship. It is good for me to hear these things and to have conversations about faithfulness with a more finely tuned articulation.

Then, we met up with a young peregrino from the Netherlands, a public prosecutor on leave to walk the Camino. Not only did I learn the distinction between Holland and the Netherlands and the history behind them but also the current reality of a country dealing with the most liberal drug laws in Europe. She works with the dark side of such freedom. When I asked, she said she is walking for "adventure, to meet new people, freedom." She also said, "Though I no longer practice, the Catholic in me enjoys the history and the churches of the tradition." When she learned I was a pastor, we had a conversation about the Dutch Reformed tradition to which her mother belongs. And then she carried on. We walked for nearly 18 miles across the high plains in beauty but intense sun. One last thing: when I arrived at our albergue, several peregrinos whom I had not seen in a few days greeted me with great enthusiasm, "Hola, Roy!" That is such a warm, wonderful greeting! One peregrino from Argentina whom I walked with many days ago said, "Roy, you are famous along the Camino. Your reputation goes ahead of you." My jaw dropped with astonishment. Then, I washed my shirt and underwear and put down my sleep sack on the bed where I'm sleeping for free. It's the two-week mark. After 218 miles, I feel good. Thanks be to God.

**Day 15 (Self-control)**
Boadmillia del Camino to Carrión de los Condes. 24.6K (15.2 miles).

We began at 6:45 a.m., walking along the Canal del Castilla, a path that is nearly identical to my beloved 184-mile Columbus & Ohio Canal towpath back home. The birds sang to us as we walked along, last evening's full moon still in view. Just lovely. We then took the alternate route along the river and completed the walk under fairly intense heat along the roadside. (It's worth noting that 15 miles is now an "easy" walk.) Today's word is *enkrateia* (self-control), the last in the list of the Fruit of the Spirit. I'm realizing in a fresh way that *enkrateia* is about the capacity for self-regulation, the ability to self-differentiate, maintain healthy boundaries, and be responsive rather than reactive. "Self-control" is usually only associated with restraint of unwanted desires. My traveling companion and I had a fascinating conversation about family systems, reframing *self-control* as this capacity to be differentiated and a sign of a mature spiritual life. Along the Camino, you bump into your personal fears, anxieties, and tendencies toward codependency. This pilgrimage is a great way to increase the capacity for healthy self-regulation. As we entered the town, we discovered that there are nearly no rooms for us. Full! We did find a place eventually, more expensive than usual but great for a nice rest.

I ended the afternoon with a shower and a beer at the local peregrino bar, sharing more conversation with Dirk, a German man who is trying to walk the Camino after quitting last year with severe blisters and shin splints. Dirk shared his positive experience in a German Catholic congregation, along with his doubts that the current pope will be allowed to change enough that is necessary for true renewal. I attended a Peregrino Mass/Eucharist tonight that moved me to tears in large part because of the singing of the Sisters of Teresa of Avila. It was contemporary music with guitar (we use the same in our worship) and concluded with a blessing and the laying on of hands by the sisters after every country present was named, over twenty. It's wonderful to experience the universal community of faith. To my great delight, I reconnected with the Japanese man who I met on the train from France and walked with on the first day (I wish I knew his name; he speaks virtually no English, but he smiles a lot!) **My legs are strong. My feet are well. My heart is full. Thanks be to God.**

**Day 16 (patience and kindness)**
Carrión de los Condes to Sahagún. 40K (24.8 mi.).

My guidebook describes this as one the most difficult stretches of the whole Camino. I agree completely. I would have to say this was the most difficult stretch on the walk. We started at 5:45 AM under the full moon and enjoyed the sunrise. Imagine walking across Nebraska for 18 miles and then along the roadside. Brutal. But, crazy me, I pushed it a little bit further and went 6 miles more because I didn't want to sit around in a little albergue all afternoon in sweltering heat. I am so grateful for my marathon running and training. The mental habits of long-distance running are really helping me on these long stretches over the high plains. I walked much of the day with my nurse practitioner peregrina, a great friend though we walked in silence. We shared some wonderful conversations over the past four days, but she decided to stay behind and rest for a day when I went on. The heat and the distance are grueling right now for many.

I've heard of so many serious foot problems, especially blisters! Some are experiencing dehydration and even sun sickness. I will be glad when this stretch is over! I arrived in my final destination but got lost trying to find the Benedictine monastery where I am staying. Totally frustrated, I finally flagged a police car. They took me right to the albergue provided by the Benedictine nuns whose community is committed to helping reduce infant poverty in Peru through the funds earned operating this place for pilgrims. I went to their singing of evening prayer and blessing for pilgrims at 7:00 p.m. and communal meal at 7:30 p.m. I'm seeing a new group of people now and only one that I started with, my pal Oscar from South Africa. It's the way of the Camino, these fluid relations. I find it a bit strange. My normal pattern is to be "best friends forever!" with most anyone I meet. That doesn't happen here. The day has been a very long and demanding. I'm glad we got a surprising bit of rain tonight. My prayer focus/chant for the next few days is on the attributes of love in I Corinthians 13; patience and kindness today.

**Day 17 (Love 2)**
Sahagún to Mansilla de las Mulas 35K (21 mi.)

I began the day walking with Oscar. The sky was beautiful with a faint rainbow, which of course is always a good sign. We walked in the rain for a couple of hours; such a contrast to yesterday's heat! I had a delightful few hours of conversation with a young peregrino from England, Mark. (By the way, most everyone I talk with is younger than I am with few exceptions.) He said he was walking the Camino to let go of his ego and allow his soul to lead him. "I want to discover myself and learn to be sufficient," he said, as if channeling Thoreau. When Oscar "outed me" as a pastor, Mark was very eager to ask me all kinds of questions, about my own practice but also about larger things, including (of all things!) the Trinity. It was great when we talked about the distinction between religion and spirituality. He was utterly surprised to hear a fresh way of living in the Spirit. He had no experience of a Christian practice that was lively or relevant to his life and is now so wonderfully curious! Mark and I talked about Western culture, England, and the U.S. All in all, we had one of those remarkable conversations that happen out here on the Camino. *He and I agreed that it's a bit like dropping into Narnia.*

Before the day ended, I had another conversation with a young (see the age theme!) peregrina from Denmark, Edna, who is walking the Camino for her gap year before she begins college. She started in Burgos a few days ago and already has blisters. When I urged her to tend to them NOW, she politely brushed me off. I told her about moleskin and said that she needed to use it if she planned to continue. I hope she heard me. Just one more thing: from Burgos to León is grueling. There are few towns along the way that have any reason to stay. It's mostly closed-up churches and ghost towns. This is why I continue to walk, when my feet are fine and my legs strong. Tomorrow, I arrive in the city of León. *Ultreia*!

Postscript to day 17. This must to be shared as a slice of the diverse life on the Camino. Around 8 p.m., as I was finishing dinner at a table outside, Oscar and I were joined by a merry band of peregrinos who wanted to share their pasta and merriment with us. The band seemed to gather around the energy of Rebecca, a young woman who is walking the Camino before pursuing an MBA/MPH degree at Yale. She started walking alone on May 24 and has walked 40K a day (25 miles), picking up these guys as she goes, Gabe, from LA, who ended a four-year Marine duty term and is now unemployed; Stephen of Shreveport, who will join the Army next month; Mauro, an Argentinian living in Barcelona without a job; and Logan, a college student from TN studying in Spain, who is traveling with his hanging sleeping bag because he sleeps out somewhere every night. Each is walking for a reason not entirely clear to me other than adventure. With the pasta they made in the nearby albergue came wine and wine and more wine. As one bottle went down, another came out. I said "I carry water," and they laughed as yet another bottle of wine came out. The utter revelry was crazy. And sure enough that herb that Americans so appreciate came forth as their merriment continued. Rebecca orchestrated the festivities with her energy, jokes, and alcohol-fueled bravado. This was a Jack Kerouac moment straight out of a hippie movie. At 2 a.m., as I slept with my ear-plugs securely in, they were going strong in the street, waking up my roommates. At 8 this morning, we came across Logan sleeping in his bag between the trees three miles from town. How he walked there after such merriment is a wonder to me.

**Day 18 (Love 3)**
Mansilla de las Mulas to León 18K (11 mi.)

This was a short and unattractive walk into the city of León, where I'll spend a couple of days resting and enjoying this city founded in 29 CE(!). My guide book encouraged one "splurge" at the Hostal San Marcos, a 15th century hospital for pilgrims now restored as a Parador Hotel and featured in *The Way*. It's a nice treat after a tough stretch, and those who have wondered if I'm going to take a rest day will be pleased. Museums, art, good food, music, and history are all here. AND I was welcomed by a nice little bird (Spanish chickadee) with whom I shared some nuts. Today, it occurred to me that walking the Camino is a world education. I've learned much about the contemporary political crisis in South Africa; the history of the Netherlands, Belgium, and Holland; German economics; the distinct regions of Spain, Castilla, Catalonia; and more. I'm so grateful to learn from my fellow peregrinos from all over the world. Listening to their experiences and different perspectives is very good for expanding my own understanding and practice. León at night is quite ALIVE! The streets are filled with people strolling around, and the cafes are standing room only. Such a lively community! The Europe Cup championship game between Barcelona and Italy brought out the whole city. (Barcelona won--and I had some great paella!) The prayer/meditation continues on the attributes of Love in I Corinthians 13. (Today = Not self-seeking)

The snail was slowly moving along the Camino with all his belongings on his back.

**Day 19 (Love 4)**
León.

A full day in the amazing city of León. I begin each day on the Camino with this prayer/chant: *"I receive this day with gratitude and an open heart."* Then, I watch for what will happen. Well, today that meant beginning with a slip in the hotel shower and severely bruising my right knee. (They don't have rubber mats in European hotels.) I iced it immediately, elevated it, and took ibuprofen. Then, I found a *farmacia* open to buy a compression wrap for the knee. I believe I'll be okay for walking tomorrow. What happened next? The city of León is celebrating Corpus Christi Day, which means a procession throughout the city with bands and hundreds of people that eventually made its way to the Cathedral of León, where the bishop welcomed everyone, including peregrinos. Hundreds of people assembled in the sanctuary filled with grand organ music.

This was also first communion, so the parade/processional included many very cute little girls and boys dressed in white Sunday clothes and their proud parents. The boys wore what appeared to be sailor suits. So much Catholic Spanish joy and pathos in the music! My pal Oscar took my photo in the pulpit of the Cathedral of León! I doubt that will happen again since I stepped around a locked gate to get there! How could I not? The children then followed my example, and I made my way out into the packed plaza. I sat in a café with my leg elevated, accompanied by my dear companions Oscar, Jess, Cecil, Mark, and Chris (who made it to León this morning). Wonderful people watching! I found the famous Casa de Botines of Antoni Gaudi (1893); all in all, a good day on a gimpy knee. Tonight, we're going to have a reunion of several of us who have now merged again in León, a street festival with wine tasting, and then wandering the old city for tapas. This is the last city before Santiago. I'm receiving this day with gratitude and an open heart. What a great evening in León with my multinational peregrino traveling crew.

**Day 20 (Love 4)**
León to Villar de Mazarife 21.5K (13.4 mi.)

This was a short walk from León, and most of it was on the road and just not so attractive, plus walking in the heat is not so fun on the feet either. We are slowly leaving the hot Meseta (high plains). Tomorrow will be the prelude to the Cantabrian Mountains. I am trying to stay in the moment, and yet, honestly, I've got my eye on the mountains! What about today? What gifts have I received? (I'm learning to ask that question every day.) I walked on a sore and swollen knee. When I arrived at the albergue, my knee needed a good rest. Lo and behold, there was a couple from Oregon also staying there. As we talked on the porch, she told me she was a doctor and would examine my obviously swollen knee. She determined there is no structural damage but a great deal of fluid. It gets better: the owner of the simple little Albergue, Pepe, is a massage therapist and has some knowledge of physical therapy. So Pepe worked on my knee with some great skill though painful because he massaged the most painful point of impact. Then he tapped the knees, asked me to walk a bit, and tapped some more. My knee is already better and much more stable than with a simple wrap. I am grateful.

I later learned that Pepe survived cancer a few years ago and as a consequence has committed his life to making this albergue a spiritually welcome place for all pilgrims as a sign of his gratitude for being cancer free. I'm told he also makes the best paella in the region. I'll confirm tonight with my friends from Portland. The American doctor has retired from medical practice to be a Spiritual Director particularly focused on Ignatian spiritual practice. Her husband is also involved in Ignatian practice.

Interestingly, they are both finding the Camino to be unsettling physically and spiritually. We agreed that folks don't often talk about the serious physical challenge. They had to give up at one point at take a bus. My only comment is that prior training is very helpful, but it doesn't fully prepare one for what actually happens out here on the Camino. These are the gifts that I have received this day, and for them I am grateful. For those who wonder about how to keep some kind of focus other than daydreaming while walking these distances, I have now memorized I Corinthians 13, made some chants, and hope that love will be more present in me. (This is a photo of Pepe, who tended my bruised knee with such kindness and skill. He owns Albergue San Antonio de Padua. On to Astorga early this morning.)

Susan Robbins Etherton sent me this poem on day 20.

**Unfolding Light**
By Steve Garnaas-Holmes
Your prayers are not little,
they are the cries of God.
Your power is not slight, it is the sun in your heart.
Your path is not through a city of strangers, but through heaven.
You are walking neither on air nor earth but on the hands of angels.
God is not far off, but within.
You are not alone, but surrounded by love.
This world is the bread, this moment the chalice.
This visible world is a window into the glorious world within it.
This is not the last chapter. There is more.

## Day 21
Villar de Mazerife to Astorga 31.5 K (19.5 mi.)

This is the three-week mark, and I have now walked 320 miles. (Without boasting and in true sympathy with my fellow peregrinos, I can say that I am grateful that I have not yet had a blister. My feet are fine, and my knee is much better. Thank you Pepe and God.) The Camino has finally moved off the flat Meseta region into the foothills of the Cantabrian Mountains. It was great to walk among trees and grasses and flowers again. I walked mostly alone but along the way had fascinating conversations with peregrinos from New Zealand and South Africa (Johannesburg), the latter telling me that she could take this walk because she has opened 12 coffee shops in the last year! (Oscar was impressed!) The former described how the last few days, she has been cutting her blisters open with scissors, putting alcohol into the incision, and then tapping. Hardcore! She did mention that she wished the alcohol were drinkable when the operation occurs! She passed me by with a spring in her step. During these stretches of walking alone, I've been creating simple prayer chants/songs that go with my current theme (Love). This has not only been fun but it's also a great way to keep the heart and mind paying attention and positive. I record the chants on my phone so that when I leave this parallel universe, I will remember. Maybe my musician friends Susan Clearman or Jeff Doenges will make them sing-able when I return. Either way, I have found it to be a new contemplative practice. I must say that as many times as I have heard and preached I Corinthians 13 on love, it's been great to walk with it these past several days. It's now there in the background of every encounter along the Camino. This afternoon, I'll visit museums in this fine small city, and tonight, I'll see my friend Lorena, who has been participating in search parties for the American woman who disappeared from the Camino in early April. It's a sad venture, but hope springs eternal.

## Day 22
Astorga Rain/Rest Day.

In between periods of rain (and hail!), I wandered around this remarkable city that dates back to 249 AD (based on letters recovered from St. Cyprian who was bishop in the wider region.) It is likely that this was a major Celtic Christian community "back in the day" and not unlikely that Paul and James preached here at some time. The city was taken over by the Visigoths in the 5th Century, then destroyed by Muslim raiders in 714, then regained stature in the 9th century. It prospered from then on and hosted more pilgrim hospitals (hostals) than any other save Burgos. One of them hosted St. Francis on his pilgrimage in 1214. Such history! There are three fine museums here, the Cathedral &

Museum, the Palacio Gaudi, and yes, the Museum of Chocolate! Astorga has been a center of chocolate in Spain since Cortés brought the cacao bean from Mexico. The Cathedral museum houses some wonderful ancient manuscripts from as early as the 10th century. What a great way to spend a rainy/rest day on the Camino.

Among all the beauty and history, I was particularly moved by my guidebook description of a 14th century cell attached to Iglesia de Santa Maria that was used to imprison prostitutes. Passing pilgrims would hand food through the bars as an act of charity. I saw the inscription still barely visible: "Remember how I was judged, for your judgment will be the same. Yesterday to me, tomorrow to you." Among the gifts of this day was another of the providential encounters that seem to happen with surprising and unpredictable regularity. A couple of days ago, I had an important conversation with a peregrina, and apparently, what I said had a significant influence on her. When I bumped into her and her husband in this city at the precise moment they stopped, drenched, in the office of tourism where I "happened" to stop for directions to the museum, she told me of her renewed courage. These things really do happen. The day ended with a rich conversation with an Australian peregrino who stopped here to see a doctor for blisters. I'm grateful for the gifts of these conversations and the people. Tomorrow, I walk again, heading toward Galicia and the mountains.

**Day 23 (Love 6)**
Astorga to Foncebadón (25.9K, 16.1 miles)

A good steady uphill walk toward the mountains of Galicia. The terrain of Northern Spain has changed, and I'm glad. (Paulo Coelho writes about this little village.) We are walking among trees and scrub bushes with the hills in the distance; flowers line a path that is rocky again. I walked the day alone. It occurred to me that walking the Camino is about more than the beauty (I have walked in many beautiful places all over the world). It's about the people, the physical challenge, the unknown, and, in my case, prayer. I have so enjoyed the people I've met from all over the world and the conversations that are engendered by this experience. From them I have learned so much. Americans (and American Christians) are isolated from the rest of the world; here, we are not. My life AND my pastoral vocation are enriched by this wide experience. The physical challenge is no small thing. Seriously, walking 790K (490 miles) is a big deal! In my case, I plan to walk 875K (543 miles) to Finisterre (the end of the world). I've been surprised at the numbers of peregrinos who have not trained for such a pilgrimage or considered the wear on their bodies. My Merrell shoes began to know my feet six months before this walk. Any blisters would have occurred long ago. My Keen sandals have been happy with my toes for a long time. Those who get their shoes a few weeks before the walk and ignore the advice to get at least a 1/2 size larger risk big problems. Even without the feet issues, walking every day for 15 to 18 miles (or more) is a challenge. Books don't talk about this enough. (Those who take bus/taxi and/or send their packs ahead are doing their Camino differently and have different perspective.)

I love the notion that "everyone walks his/her Camino." I can only speak of my own Camino. So how about the sleeping? I've stayed in the least expensive albergues and the most expensive hotels and everything in between. I've put my sleeping sack on a mat on the floor, and I've put it on a bunk in a room shared with 50 or more. I've shared a two-bed room and I've shared a room with six bunk beds. I've paid five euros, and I've paid forty-five euros. There are many sleeping accommodations, but I prefer the smaller ones, and I always have my earplugs and my sleep. This is part of living with the unknown on the Camino. (But I must say, as more people walk, there is a greater tendency for people to reserve a place to stay, which puts pressure on those like me who have no phone service or simply want to walk into town in the original way.) Living with the unknown has been a gift for me on the Camino. I fear and I love it. I think this must be close to living by faith. At the end of each day, I wash my shirt and underwear and hang them out to dry. On the good advice of my wife, I've been wearing a long-sleeved shirt for sun protection. I only need one shirt when I wash it every day! We concluded this day with a mass/Eucharist offered in a very small, ancient church by a priest from Mississippi walking the Camino. Peregrinos from France, Cuba, Spain, the Netherlands, Canada (Quebec), Germany, South Africa, and the United States attended. Then, I had a delightful conversation with a peregrino from Quebec. I'm grateful for this day.

This evening, I went to the Cruz Ferro, the traditional highest point of the Camino at 4,500 feet. This was once an ancient Celtic site. For centuries, pilgrims have brought a stone or something of symbolic importance to represent a burden they are leaving at the cross, a tall wooden pole topped by an iron cross. I came alone at sunset because I wanted to miss crowds who gather and because the light is wonderful.

**Day 24 (Love 6)**
Foncebadón to Ponferrada 27 K (16 mi.)

The first part of the walk was a beautiful gradual ascent to the Cruz de Ferro (Iron Cross) at sunrise. It was 37°F in the mountains (hills) and I loved it! Oscar, my steady traveling companion, left at 6 a.m. for a mass held at the cross. I left later and walked the day alone, which is fine. Along the way, I sang my chants and prayed for people. It was also great to be in a higher altitude. The descent was pretty brutal on the knees! I arrived in this city that was once a Celtic outpost and later famous for the huge Knights of Templar castle, which I toured with a couple of peregrinos from Quebec and Arizona. The old city is really delightful, with plazas and cafes where people (like me) drink their favorite beverages, eat olives, and have conversations. I continue to note the number of people walking this way who describe themselves as non-practicing Catholics; they go to mass at every occasion and say their Camino is about self-discovery. I think we Christians need new language to talk about this yearning for deeper self-understanding. My Camino is about fully listening, with clarity and without judgment, as folks describe what moves them to walk 500 miles on an ancient pilgrim path. Just their story is a marvel and sometimes a clue to the work of the Spirit in our time. Then the other side of my brain says this is the 60s-70s in a new key. And that's worth noting too, without judgment. Buen Camino!

**Day 25 (Love 7)**
Ponferadda to Villafranca. 24K (15 mi.)

Today was one of those days in which I decided to change plans as unexpected gifts came my way. Oscar left early and walks much faster than I do. Usually, we meet at our destination. Today, I came upon three college students from the Netherlands and decided that I wanted hear their stories, share mine, and get to know them rather than rush ahead. They stopped for mid-day (10 a.m.) lunch, something I never do. So I walked on but within minutes realized that I didn't want to pass up the gift of getting to know these young people. I turned around and sat with them for their lunch. We carried on together. It was delightful. I got to hear why they consider themselves non-religious and share my own sharp critique of religion and commitment to a practice more personal, lively, and challenging. They found that astonishing and actually helpful. They are majoring in economics and government, so we had this great comparison of our countries. Then, we talked some about the Dutch Reformed tradition and its current practice in the Netherlands. All of which I would have missed if I had passed up the opportunity. For me, these encounters are so important out here on the Camino when so many are rushing. We arrived at Villafranca 1.5 hours later than my normal pace. Oscar decided to go on.

Now, I'm sharing a simple room for four in an albergue in a 17th century church, Iglesia de San Nicolás el Real. (That means tomorrow I'll be walking 20 miles up over the mountain rather than 14 with rain predicted, but I'm glad for my decision.)

Villafranca is described as one of the most beautiful towns on the Camino. It's just below a mountain pass over into Galicia at the confluence of rivers Burbia and Valcarce. I leisurely explored the town, walking the narrow streets and visiting the church that legend has it Saint Francis founded on this pilgrimage in the 12th century. It's market day! The ancient hospital Santiago is also here. Pilgrims who were sick would pass through the doors and receive pardon, relieving them of the strenuous last stage to Santiago. It is a rare opportunity to soak in this history of a county that merges with the history of Christianity. I'm sad to say that it appears all that is left of the living Church are these buildings that have become museums, mostly closed. I walked along the river where homes with coats of arms from the 17th century still stand. At the end of the day, I sat at a plaza cafe writing this post with a glass of wine and a small bowl of olives, watching the townspeople and peregrinos come out from their siesta to the plaza for tapas. Tonight, I will eat salmon at the albergue with my young friends from the Netherlands. My life is blessed, and I'm grateful to receive this day with gratitude and an open heart.

**Day 26 (Love 8)**
Villafranca to O Cebriero 30K (20 miles)

This day began in the dark predawn with disappointment because I missed the alternative route over the mountains. I am directionally challenged, especially in the dark! So I spent the better part of the morning letting go of that mistake. Then, I began to reframe my situation and a series of thoughts followed, beginning with this: pay attention to the beauty where I am rather than where I could have been or should have been. That was a helpful way to receive the day and gradually let go of the disappointment. Then, it occurred to me that I was prepared for rain all day, and it didn't rain at all while I was walking. So that's a reason to be grateful. But the most unexpected and great gift of the day happened at the last two miles of a steep ascent, when I came alongside a high school student from Michigan who said he was "discerning a call to the priesthood" and very confused. He is with a group of students and a couple of priests. We had a rich conversation about the process of discernment and how small steps matter a lot. I was filled with gratitude knowing this is the reason I missed my original route. I arrived at O Cebriero, high and beautiful, in Galicia and will stay at the public albergue with 100 other peregrinos. This not my favorite experience but definitely a part of walking the Camino. It's raining and cold. I've spent the afternoon taking with peregrinos from Australia, Minneapolis, Hungary, Indiana, and San Francisco. It's still raining, but I'm warm and dry. I'm walking alone again, as my pal has gone on ahead. I will receive each day with gratitude.

**Day 27**
Foggy day.

I walked most of the day in the fog at high altitude, but that is no excuse for getting momentarily lost again. I walked a quarter mile past my turn mile when I realized I was not on the Camino. Luckily, I managed to flag down a car. The driver graciously took me back to the Camino. (In all fairness, sometimes an albergue puts a yellow arrow down to direct walkers to their place rather than the Camino, and that's why I passed by. Still, folks laughed!) So I walked in the fog, which was wonderful in its own way. Walking in fog is a great way to meditate on faith because so much of life (at least my life) is in fog. Karl Barth described faith this way. All in all, it was an excellent day. I had a conversation with an American couple and later with a peregrino from Austin, Cheryl, with whom I had a lively conversation about spirit and more. What a great friend! Then I met Hadar from Tel Aviv, my first Israeli companion on the Camino. This concludes another day. [By the way, I'm staying in a much better albergue tonight, less crowded and very clean. Nice gift.]

**Day 28**
Triacastela to Morgade 37K (23 mi.)

What a delightful day of walking! The Camino went through the woods and along the river in early morning fog. Again, birds serenaded us as we passed through Galician farms. I walked in the morning with a peregrina from Austin, Texas, a mother of two daughters, a certified master gardener, an artist who runs a bed and breakfast (brew and breakfast), and a former massage therapist, who has studied Tibetan Buddhism for twelve years. (I'm telling you what she told me!) She took great delight in regaling me with stories of her experience with Buddhism, dreams, and much more as we walked through this beautiful land, frequently dropping the F bomb with great zest. I just walked along, listening and laughing, and thinking this listening is very good for me. I don't think she has any idea of my vocation. We walked until Sarria at 11 miles, when she stopped for a beer and rest. I carried on alone for 9 miles through the same farmlands, along lanes lined with ancient stonewalls until I reached Morgade. My guidebook lists the population as four! They must all run the nice albergue in this enchanting place. Once I settled in, I had a conversation with a Polish man, living in Ontario, who told me that he left his Camino for 4 days to fly back to Poland to receive the Silver Medal for his work with the Solidarity movement in the '80s. He is a nuclear scientist who had to flee Poland in those days because of his political work. Now, he is known for both science and Solidarity in Poland. Remarkable. Then, the famous merry band of young (hippie) travelers from several days back--

Rebecca, Logan, and Mauro, with a few others--showed up! We had a happy Camino-style reunion; so glad to see them this close to Santiago. I concluded this evening by dining with walkers from Switzerland, Canada (British Columbia), and Poland. The Canadians acknowledged their atheism and were curious about my own Camino. We had a very good exchange. These encounters are so rich for me. I'm grateful as I watch the sun set on another day. "I receive this day in gratitude and an open heart." It never stops coming, and I want to stay open.

**Day 29 (Faith and Freedom)**
30K (18.6 mi.)

I began walking early (before sunrise). When you go to bed at 10 p.m., lights out in the albergue, it's easy to wake early. I love walking alone in the predawn quiet along these country lanes as the roosters crow, the dogs snooze, and the birds sing. The Camino is now fully in the Galicia region where the hórreos are prominent. (Hórreos are granaries unique to this region and Southern Portugal.) (See photo) I first thought it was a burial site! No. Being in Galicia, I began thinking of the Apostle Paul and his letter to the Galatians. (Not the same region but still calls to mind Galatians!) Anyway, faith and freedom are the keys to that letter, and they go with life in the Spirit, which has been a central meditation on my Camino. The apostle said freedom means, "bearing one another's burden" (Galatians 6:1-2). I have certainly experienced this on the Camino; bearing another's burden is happening nearly every day. Faith has become a daily practice of openness and attention. Walking among these Galician farmers makes me imagine them hearing Paul's counsel about life in the Spirit that goes far beyond the bounds of religion. I'm guessing that the freedom of life in the Spirit (as I understand it) is what many people walking the Camino want, including me, even if we describe that longing differently.

One more thing: it's a bit disconcerting to be joined now by lots of people walking who come by bus/taxi only to walk the final 100K to Santiago. Someone referred to them as "tourgrinos," or in the case of celebrities who do this (yes they do), as "celegrinos." (I don't want to be harsh, but there should be some other category for folks who walk the Camino in this way.) When I arrived at my albergue after 19 miles, I kindly asked my hospitalira if I could have a bottom bunk rather than one of the remaining two top bunks. She winked at me, smiled, and showed me to a different room with only two beds. I'm grateful and blessed and receive the day. (See photo) It is 70K (43.5 miles) to Santiago.

# I Surrender

*created by Roy W. Howard during his walk along the Camino de Santiago, summer 2015*

*transcribed and harmonized by Jeff Doenges*

1. Oh, I sur-ren-der, Oh, I sur-ren-der, I sur-ren-der my heart to you that your love may grow in me that your love may grow in me.

©2016

**Day 29**
Portos to Aruzia 34 K (21 mi.)

As the Camino gets closer to Santiago, it moves through urban and suburban areas with occasional country lanes. This is difficult in many ways, not the least of which is the tourists who have descended on the way. Sadly, they are loud and often obnoxious. I walk in a higher gear to pass them by and have a bit of the Camino alone. Along with this roadside walking comes a bit of physical and emotional weariness that I have to set aside. But the little bird that has been serenading me for weeks finally stopped long enough for me to take his photo. That orange chest! (Look closely on the tree with the arrow.) Today, I was recalling that hospital for sick pilgrims in Ponferrada. When the pilgrims crossed through the door, their indulgences for sins were covered, and thus, they didn't have to walk all the way. This sort of pilgrimage to remove sins led to the Reformation! I have no idea how many people are doing their Camino to gain indulgence for sins, but I haven't talked with any, and I doubt it's very many. I'm actually walking for another reason: to experience the Spirit of God in fresh ways in the lives of the people, to discern what may be a new reformation occurring among people for which we need new language and new forms. This walking among people from so many cultures is an opportunity to perceive the love of God manifest in strikingly new ways. I put no limits on this appearance of Love; why should I?

My songs help me as I walk, imagining I am walking among new pilgrims in a new reformation that will burst the boundaries of what is now known. One of my songs has this refrain: "Deeper and deeper we walk into the love of God for us./Praying for others as we walk into the love of God for us./Loving our neighbors as we walk into the love of God for us." And so on. I have 24 miles to go to Santiago and expect to enter the city early Saturday morning.

**Day 30**
Aruzia to Lavacolla 32K (19.8 mi.)

A modest walk mostly along roadways and through farm land and country lanes lined with Eucalyptus trees. Though I walked much of this six-hour trek alone, I did travel for a while with a young man from Chicago who is walking with his uncle before he starts nursing school at University of Arizona in the fall. They started on the primitive Camino, which is a rugged branch over the mountains that merges with the Camino de Santiago. We commiserated about the horrible massacre in Charleston.

I asked him why he was walking, and he said, "I need to be away from America for a while. I don't know; I want to be better, less competitive. Everything is so driven. I want to be a more solid person." "What do you mean by 'solid'?" I asked.
"I want to be more fair, I guess that's right, more fair, especially with my parents. I'm not good to them. I want to be more kind and less mean. Yeah, that's it: I want to be less mean." "Are you walking for religious reasons?"
He was emphatic. "No! Definitely no."

During the early morning, I walked with my friend Karine from Quebec. She grew up on her family farm where her parents and brother still work. Karine has college degrees and works with cattle as an 'inseminator.' "I give life to bulls and cows," she said with a smile. She had told me many days ago that she was Catholic but "non-religious, not practicing." I shared with her that Dietrich Bonhoeffer wrote that whatever survives of the faithful Church after WWII will have no language that is respected by a "religion-less society" because it had lost integrity from the *nazification* of the tradition. Bonhoeffer said those who survive (he sadly didn't) will have "to practice the arcane discipline of silence, prayer, and acts of compassion; perhaps a new language will emerge that will speak to a religion-less people" for whom God is dead. I asked Karine if she thought Bonhoeffer was right, as I most certainly do. She replied, wide-eyed and smiling, "Yes! Yes. I've never heard this but I think it is true. I have nothing to do with religion, but I believe and have sensed God on my journey." I asked her what that means, and that prompted a longer conversation!

One last thing: she has not stayed in a hotel for the whole Camino, but on this stretch, there is a hotel that is in Lavacolla, which translated means "Wash private parts." Here, the traditional pilgrims, who did not bathe on their journey, stopped just before Santiago to be clean before entering the city and Cathedral. With a friendly boldness that comes from this journey, she asked if she could share a room with me. Since we have been staying in various communal arrangements for a month, it makes perfect sense. So we share a hotel room and she has the chance to freshen up for our great day tomorrow! One more last thing: it's a simple pleasure at the end of a day of walking to have the ritual of washing my clothes as well as my body, then hanging them to dry in the warm breeze. Then a beer or wine and salad, today accompanied by pulpo (octopus) the specialty of Galicia region. Every day, I've worn the bracelet my daughter gave me. I'm so glad to say it has survived with me on this whole journey. It has meant a lot to me, along with the affection and prayers of the people and love of my wife and family. Santiago is five miles away.

**Day 31**
Lavacolla to SANTIAGO DE COMPOSTELA! 10K (6 miles)

I walked into Santiago with Karine at 9 a.m. Jess Kennedy and her dear friend Cecil were so kind to welcome us as we walked into the Cathedral square! Wow. What a moment. I cried with laughter and gratitude after these 800K (497.1 miles). I then greeted others with whom I've shared this long, wondrous Camino, some that I shared stories and sleeping quarters with and others with whom I've simply shared smiles and understanding. Then, I met up with the two German guys that I started with 31 days ago and walked with for so many days, Simon and Holger! Oscar is here with his wife, who flew in to greet him, as well as Marrissa and her father Brad from Portland! After greeting so many, I went to the noon mass at the Cathedral. Again I cried with gladness at this worship because I sensed how astonishing it is that hundreds of local people and peregrinos from around the world are experiencing this moment. I sat in a pew with peregrinos from Canada, Poland, France, Slovakia, and South Korea. The lessons and prayers were read in several languages, including English (by a peregrino priest from Mississippi with whom I walked). I also experienced again the unifying power of the common Eucharist liturgy because though I didn't follow all the Spanish, I knew the liturgical movements well enough to join with all these fellow pilgrims sharing many languages. Pentecost. This is one humanity united in the Spirit in the Eucharist. (Yes, though I am not Roman Catholic, I receive communion. It's so right.) Then, the great ritual of the *Botofumeria* occurred; the gathered people receive the blessings of the incense in this grand movement where the huge sensor is swung by rope through the sanctuary.

Karine started walking the next stage to Finisterre-Muxia on the coast after the worship! I will greet friends today and have dinner with others this evening, including Chris and Mark from Quebec, Jerneja from Slovenia, Alexandra from Poland, Oscar and Emilene from South Africa, and Marissa and Brent from Portland. Then, I believe I will begin my walk to Finisterre-Muxia tomorrow (or perhaps Monday). My life is blessed to be a blessing, and I am filled with gladness and gratitude. I am remembering my Camino friends still walking, especially Debbie, Jeff, Janet, Aaron, Judith, Logan, Judy, Louise, Lorena, Cheryl, Caira, Misha, Leah, and more. I'm grateful for all of you who are praying for me.

The greatest thing about this (rest) day in Santiago is welcoming so many of my peregrino friends as they enter the city and complete their Camino. It's a wonderful company of international pilgrims, some of whom I have not seen since beginning this journey and including my young pals from the Netherlands; the Japanese pilgrim who helped me on the train way, way back in Paris; and Jerneja from Slovenia, merry travelers Cheryl and Rebecca; Misha; and Lynn, Peter, and Robert from my original albergue in St. Jean.

# Post-Santiago: The Way continues

**Day 33**
Santiago to Negreira 21.9K (13.6 miles)

The first stage toward the sea is an easy walk out of Santiago. Once I arrived at Negreira, I met a woman named Catherine Lee, who started running (!) the Camino de Santiago in April as a way to honor her father, who died young of a heart attack. She is running to raise money for the British Heart Foundation. We talked for a while; then, she had to run her last stretch back to Santiago. She was not a runner before this challenge. She said she wanted to do something big for her dad. What an amazing accomplishment! I made a donation and told her that her father would be proud of her. At the same café, I met Dennis, a young guy from Holland who has been walking 1000K across Germany and the Camino toward Finisterre. A fully tattooed man, he works for the Dutch border police and has six months of vacation accrued. He too donated to Catherine's cause. Two years ago, he rode a rickshaw across India to raise 48,000 euros for two orphanages in Mumbai. You never know the generous people you will meet on any given day. There are so many remarkable people out here. My post-Santiago pilgrimage continues, and I continue to receive gifts every day.

**Day 34**
Negreira to Olveiroa 33.3K (20.7 mi.)

This is the longest stage on the Finisterre route, and by day's end, my feet could tell. The temperature was 60°F all day, remarkable after days of serious heat. The Camino went through forests with a 1400-foot elevation. Yet, most of it was on hard ground, which is tough on the feet. I suppose it would be an understatement to say that I know my feet pretty well, along with my legs and especially knees. Among the highlights of this day was the moment when I walked in a small set of travelers from Holland, China, Spain, and Italy. The international character of the Camino continues to impress me! It will surprise many of those who know me well that after nearly 520 miles of walking, I decided (again) to break a pattern and listen to music while walking. I thought that this might carry me on this final stretch to the sea at the end of the earth. (I never wear earphones walking or long running. Thank you Diane Wirono for giving me special earphones for just this possibility.) I'm glad I did. In case you are curious about the music, I listened to three extraordinary songwriters' new music that I had downloaded on Spotify. Josh Garrels (*Lost Animals*), Elise Erikson Barrett (*Awake*) and Emmylou Harris (*Traveling Kind*). I had no idea how wonderfully perfect their music would be for just this journey. I'm grateful. The funniest moment: after 21 miles of walking, my friend, the police man from Amsterdam, does 50 push-ups. When I joked with him about it, he gave me a short lecture on the importance of core work for the whole body. I laughed kindly, thinking my Pilates coach would approve. Surprising moment: unexpected tears of gladness/gratitude keep occurring. Tomorrow, I hope to reach the sea at the end of the earth. Which means my last night in a 20-person albergue. What is life without earplugs?

**Day 35**
Olveiroa to Finisterre 34.6K (21.5 mi.)

I made it to "the end of the earth." I can't fully describe what it feels like to arrive here at the Lighthouse after walking 543.7 miles with all my belongings on my back. My feet are sore, my hips are happy to carry no more, and my knees are glad for rest. Yet, my mind is clear, my spirit is alive, and my heart is filled with gladness and gratitude. I celebrated at the Lighthouse with my Dutch friend, Dennis, who walked this last stretch with me. It's the 0 Kilometers mark. We burned our socks, as it is tradition to burn something, and shared a bottle of wine. What a great surprise to greet my young friends from the Netherlands who had taken a bus to Finisterre. How does such timing occur? It's holy to me. So now my Camino is done, but my journey continues. I'm staying in Muxia up the coast to rest and reflect on this incredible experience. The first thing I did was put my feet in the Atlantic Ocean! I turn now with anticipation to meet Claudia in Madrid on Saturday, and before then to greet more peregrino friends arriving in Santiago on Friday. I am so grateful that I could take this pilgrimage all the way from the mountains to the sea! Just astonished; I wept with gladness at the end. Thank you all for your prayers and words of encouragement! We are one community and the journey goes on forever for each of us. Ultreïa!

Muxia is a beautiful seaside village. Legend (yes the Spanish Catholics love legends!) has it that Saint Mary appeared here in a stone boat to deliver encouragement to a very discouraged Saint James. She told him his mission was completed and to return to Jerusalem. The church, which was struck by lightning on Christmas Day in 2013, still overlooks the ocean by the lighthouse. The stones in front are said to be from the original boat, and thousands come here in September to celebrate the event. I continue to see fellow peregrinos making their way here by foot or bus.

June 26 - On this last night in Santiago, it was so great to meet with Jeff and Janet, whom I started with in St. Jean, and Debbie Carl Freeman, whom I accompanied in the Spirit along the way. Cheryl met us for tapas after a 36-hour journey from Washington DC to Santiago.

# Epilogue

*Solvitur Ambulando*: "It is solved by walking." The problem to be solved depends on the person. After walking the Camino, I have adopted walking as an ongoing spiritual practice.

What I have discovered is that walking provides a medium for reflection, discernment, and physical delight. This can be said of other activities like running or biking. Yet, after running six marathons and numerous half marathons, I know the difference. Walking slows me down, running speeds me up. Walking compels me to consider my surroundings differently, to notice things as I pass and become more mindful. I experience the earth differently when I am walking.

There is a common saying: *The Camino begins when the Camino ends*. This has certainly been true for me. Since returning, I have continued my practice of walking, choosing to slow my life down, to arrange my schedule differently, allowing me, for instance, to walk 2.5 miles to the hospital for pastoral visits or a home for pastoral conversations. Walking, I experience the neighborhoods around our church mindfully, and even better, I know my neighbors, with whom I share stories during my walks.

*The Camino begins when the Camino ends.* This is the story of my life, and I am still trying to integrate what happened to my life along the Camino into my post-Camino experience. I can't say it has been easy, but I am making progress. Still, the desire to return remains intense.

My older daughter, knowing how much the Camino has touched my life, suggested I walk the two-day 39.3-mile Avon walk to end breast cancer. Perfect! Remarkably, she, her sister, and my wife, who is a breast cancer survivor, decided to walk. We formed a team – Walking in Love – and invited others to join us. We have raised $27,000. The 13 of us will walk a marathon (26.2 miles) on one day and a half-marathon (13.1 miles) the next. When the Camino ends, the Camino begins.

We are walking in love.

One last thing: I wanted a way to mark this experience into my body reminding me of gratitude, freedom and faith. This is why I now have a tattoo. It's a shell, an early symbol of baptism and of the original pilgrims who walked the Camino. And remember that word, Ultreïa? It's etched on my skin above the shell. My spirit is marked with the Camino. So is my body. *The Camino begins when the Camino ends*. I'm grateful. If this my experience has provoked questions about your own pilgrimage, I would be delighted to have conversation with you.

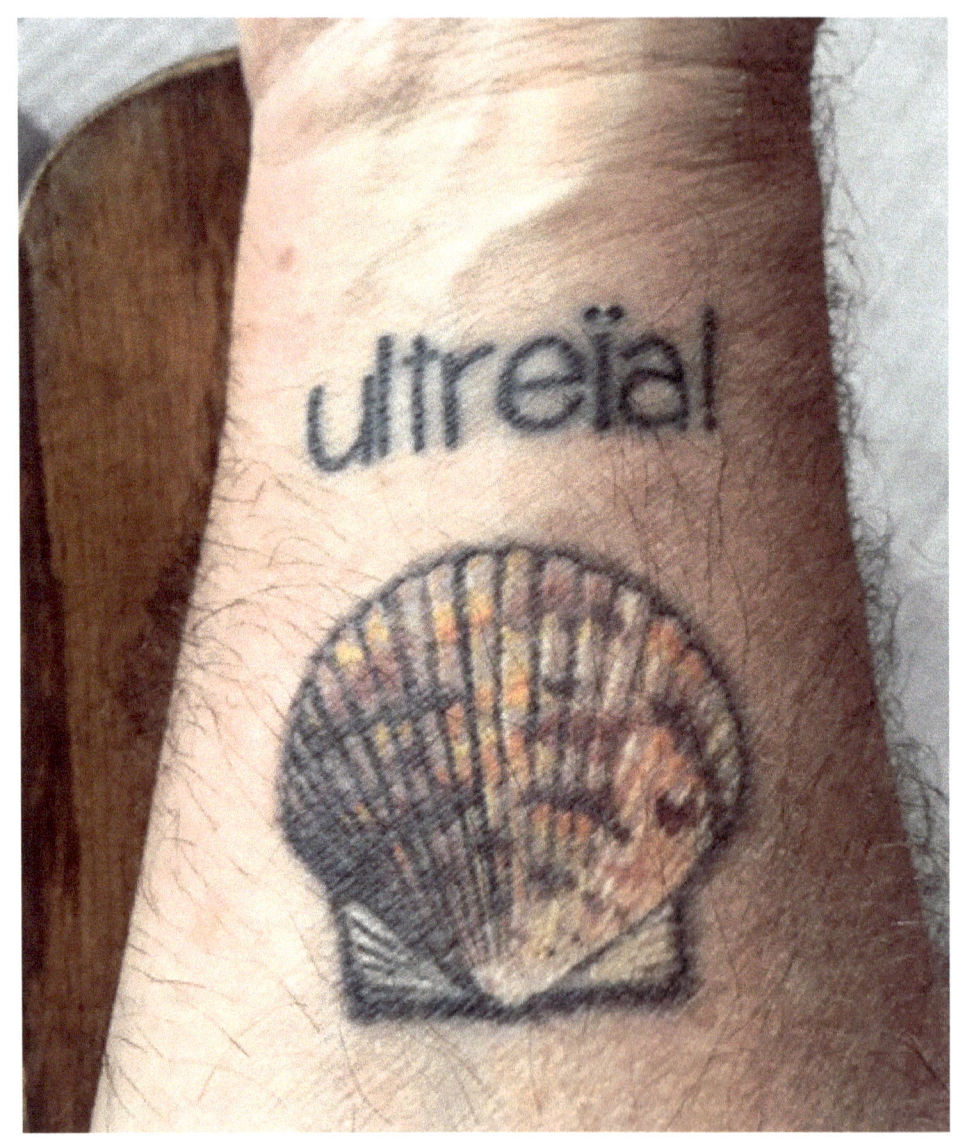

# A few of my Camino Companions

www.ingramcontent.com/pod-product-compliance
Lightning Source LLC
Chambersburg PA
CBHW051349110526
44591CB00025B/2950